Seasonal Foraging:
15 Autumn Wild Foods to Find In The Forest

The information herein is offered for informational purposes solely, and is universal as sc. The presentation of the information is without contract or any type of guarantee assurance.

Table of content

Introduction

Foraging for food requires you to look for anything which is growing in the wild. It is usual to focus around where you live, collecting items and then preparing them before eating them. This is a skill that humans have had since the dawn of humanity; foraging was historically an essential part of the diet; even the best hunters could not guarantee success on every trip. Alongside this foraging can provide a wide range of additional nutrients and minerals which are necessary to ensure a balanced diet and a healthy lifestyle.

In modern times there are two significant benefits from learning to forage properly. The most obvious of these is the ability to provide food for yourself and your family without having to pay for it. There is very little more rewarding and satisfying than knowing you have found your own food. It certainly seems to make it taste better!

The second reason is the need for survival. It is always a possibility that you will become lost in the wilderness; this could be a walking trip gone wrong or the result of an accident. It is one of those events that most people think will never happen to them and certainly one that you hope you will never have to deal with. However, having an idea about the right types of food available at different times of the years will allow you to make the most of any situation. There is always some food available so that you will not starve. The trick is to know where to look and what to do with it!

Of course, the type of food available will depend upon the region you are living in; it is important to learn about your local area and then locate the right foods for your area. At least some of the fifteen wild foods will be available near you.

Autumn is one of the best times to find food by foraging. It is the traditional harvest season and there is an abundance of items ripe ready for the picking. Although it is possible to forage throughout the entire year, autumn is definitely the most abundant time.

When foraging it is also important to note that you should not waste your time looking for items that you are either not sure about identifying properly or that you cannot easily find. Mushrooms are one of the best examples of this type of food. They grown in sunny but damp places and can be difficult to find. It can also be difficult to be certain that the mushroom you have picked is the edible one you think it is and not one that will make you poorly or even kill you. If you are not sure that you can identify each mushroom properly then you are better saving your energy and using it to forage for food that you know you can consume.

An additional benefit of foraging is that you can have a lot of fun and good exercise whilst looking for the different food types.

Chapter 1 – Five Autumn Nuts

One of the most important parts of foraging is making sure that you only take what you need. Although many of these foods can be stored effectively for extended periods of time it is essential to balance the amount you take with what you will realistically use throughout the year. This will ensure that there remain plenty of foods for other people who wish to forage and that you do not damage the environment for future foraging requirements.

It is also worth noting that whenever you are out, whether you are going to specifically forage or not, it is worth taking a pair of scissors or a good penknife. A foldable bag is also extremely beneficial as it can be carried easily with you at all times but quickly unpacked to provide a means of carrying your foraged goodies! It is also worth noting that many of the best wild foods are located in woodlands and hedges where there may be stinging nettles and thorns. It is best to wear long trousers, long sleeves and boots when foraging. You may even like to take gloves with you to ensure you are protected from the more hazardous side of nature. Many foragers also carry a note book; this can be useful to record where certain items have been found. You will find it extremely useful in future years as you will know exactly where to go for a specific food type.

Some of the most commonly found foods in autumn are nuts; these can make a delicious snack at any time of the day or can be used as a supplement in a variety of meals.

1. Hazelnuts

http://www.bestherbalhealth.com/wp-content/uploads/2014/01/Hazelnuts.jpg

This is one of the most popular nuts if you are a squirrel! You may find yourself competing with them or you may find that you have been beaten to the punch and all the hazelnuts you can find are simply shells. If this is the case then you will need to make a note to start earlier the next year!

Hazelnuts are often found along boundaries as they are a popular type of hedging. They can also be found in mixed natural woodland or are often included in community planting schemes. The first step is to ensure you can identify the leaves of this distinctive tree. You will then be able to look under the leaves to find the nuts, still in their shells. The best ones are still green. You can simply crack the shell and eat them as they are. It is worth noting that not all shells actually have a nut inside. To preserve them and eat them throughout the year you can take them home and put them in a dry, dark place. This will dry the nuts out and allow you to keep them in a sealed container throughout the year. They can be eaten dried or you can roast them, adding any flavoring you choose, to add a special zing to your hazelnuts.

2. Sweet chestnuts

The sweet chestnut is also known as the European chestnut as it originates from Europe. However, as with many species of plant it is now found in many countries around the world. In fact, there are a large number of them across the Eastern parts of the United States.

Most people will already be familiar with the trees which are generally very big. The chestnuts are hidden inside the spiky casings. You will find many casings starting to appear on the ground in the early autumn, however these will generally be from younger trees and the nuts will either be small or non-existent. If you wait until October you will find the more established trees start to drop their spiky casings. You will need to carefully break open the protective spiky casing to release the chestnut. You will then have a range of options regarding what to do with the nuts. The easiest option is to simply score them and roast them. However, if you prefer you can score them and them dip them in boiling water for a few minutes. This will allow you to peel them and you can add them to cakes, or a variety of other recipes.

3. The Beech Nut

Unsurprisingly this nut can be found on the Beech tree. This is an extremely common tree, found all around the world. It is often underappreciated and over-looked by many foragers and even commercial outlets. The nut casings will appear on the beech tree every year, however, they will only produce nuts every three years. This means you may need to try several trees before you find one which is producing nuts. It is worth remembering that two trees next to each other can be different ages and one may be producing whilst the other is not. You will need to check each one. Once you do locate a tree which is producing nuts then you will find there are hundreds of nuts to choose from.

It may appear to be difficult to extract the nut but, in fact, it is very easy! Place the beech nuts on a tray in the oven to dry roast them. After approximately half an hour you should be able to remove the hot nuts and rub them between two tea towels; the shell will simply flake off.

It is also possible to collect a large quantity of these nuts together and press them to extract their oil. Beech oil is very popular in some parts of the world.

4. Acorns

You are probably already aware of what an acorn looks like. Even if you have not seen them in the wild you will have seen them on the television in films such as Ice Age. The acorn comes from an Oak tree; there are hundreds of these all around the world; particularly in the western world. They are actually full of protein and carbohydrates making them an excellent source of energy whether to supplement your diet or as part of surviving in the wild.

However, acorns should not be eaten raw from the tree; they are full of chemicals called tannins. Whilst this is not harmful to humans it does give the acorn a bitter taste; one that is guaranteed to put most people off them for life.

Fortunately it is easy to remove the tannins from these nuts. Simply add the whole acorn; in its kernel to a pan of water and boil for fifteen minutes. The water will go brown. You then dispose of the water and boil them again. After several cycles of this the water will remain clear and the tannins will have been removed.

It is worth noting that a white acorn will only take one or two cycles whereas the red oak acorn may take six or seven changes. You should not throw the all the tannin filled water away; it can be applied to insect bites and stings to remove the irritation.

Once you have removed all the tannins the acorns actually taste delicious; you can add them to a variety of recipes, eat them raw or you can attempt to make coffee with them!

5. Walnuts

Walnut trees appear all over the northern hemisphere despite the fact they originated from the southern parts of Europe where it was traditionally warmer and more humid. A walnut tree will start to produce nuts once they are approximately fifteen years old but the best nuts can be found on trees that are thirty years or older. The average mature tree will produce fifty kilograms of nuts every year.

Walnuts are hidden behind the distinctive green covering which is notoriously difficult to remove. It is also likely to stain everything it touches. To make it easier for yourself you should pick the walnuts as they turn from bright green to a yellow color. This is when they are just becoming ripe and the squirrels will compete with you for the best ones. The ripe hull should split by itself, if it does not it can be easily split by applying pressure and the walnut will be free.

Once you have collected your nuts it is advisable to place them in a bowl of water; this will help you to sort the good ones from the bad. Bad nuts will float to the surface. Once they have been thoroughly washed you will need to dry them. If you split the shell open you will be able to leave them to air dry or even roast them but they will need to be eaten fairly quickly to avoid them spoiling. Alternatively you can leave them to dry in their shells. You must store them in a dry but dark place. If you store them properly they have been known to last for up to a year.

Chapter 2 – 5 Autumn Berries for the Avid Forager

Nuts are not the only things which can be found in abundance at this time of year. Berries are a popular choice and a nice alternative to nuts if being used as a survival food. They can also make a good mixture as a snack for parties. Berries are generally sweet and can be added to a wide variety of deserts as well as being mixed into recipes such as cakes, pies and crumbles to create a delicious, home-made and potential free desert.

Berries are usually found on plants and bushes which have thorns and even prickly leaves; this is usually a deterrent to the many animals which want to consume the berries. To avoid getting scratched all over it is advisable to wear gloves. Some of the berries will already be well known to you, whilst others are less known but delicious if you are prepared to work a little harder for your foraging goodies.

1. Blackberries

This is probably one of the first berries you will think of when you consider foraging in the autumn. In fact, you have probably already tried it at some point. The blackberry is distinctive, the only other berry that looks similar is the black raspberry which is native to America and is also edible; the only difference is the taste! It is worth considering where you pick your blackberries. Many of them grow on the edge of fields and may have been exposed to pesticides which you do not want to eat! Blackberries which are next to roads with a high volume of traffic can also be full of less than desirable substances.

To check if a blackberry is ripe you can hold the blackberry between your thumb and finger. You should be able to turn it a little and pull downwards. The berry should simply fall into your hand; if it does not it will remain attached and you can try again in a few days. A blackberry which is not yet ripe can have a sour taste and ruin the taste of your creation.

Once you have picked your blackberries it is advisable to let them soak in some lightly salted water; this will ensure any small bugs are killed off. You can then rinse them and either freeze them or use them. They can be turned into jam, chutney and even wine very easily. They can also be frozen and used in crumbles, cakes, or simply served with a little cream.

When freezing it is advisable to spread them on a tray; they will freeze individually; you can then store them in the freezer in a container or bag and you will be able to defrost just the amount you need.

2. The Sloe berry

The Sloe berry comes from the blackthorn bush and is a common sight across Europe and Northern America. The berries are fairly distinctive in that they have the appearance of a small plum. You can also tell by tasting them; they are extremely sour!

They are easy to pick, just like the blackberries they will simply drop into your hand when ripe. You will then be able to use them to make a variety of different creations. One of the most popular is to add them to some cheap gin and a little sugar. You can then leave them to ferment for several months before straining the liquid; you will have created your own sloe gin. Alternatively you can use vodka if you fancy trying sloe vodka. It is important to shake the container regularly whilst it is fermenting. The sloes retrieved from the fermenting process will be sweeter and can be used to make pies or even added to ice cream; just make sure you remove the stones first.

3. Elderberries

The elderberry tree is a common sight in many places across the northern hemisphere. It is a beautiful green tree with huge clusters of black berries. The weight
of the berries will cause the branches of the tree to hang low and create a stunning autumnal back drop. The tree is generally medium sized although young
ones will appear more like bushes but still have a favorable harvest to offer.

Elderberries are considered to be an extremely healthy wild food. They have a
large amount of vitamin C as well as an array of other vitamins and antioxidants.

The berry is sweet with a slight sour taste which makes it perfect for creating your
own wine or even vinaigrette. They make an excellent addition to any pie as they
will balance out any other berry or you can even make an elderberry jam.

Perhaps most interestingly is that the elderberry can also be used as a natural
dye. The color will obviously be a red / purple. The fact that it can be used as a
dye should forewarn you that these small berries can mark your skin for a signif-
cant period of time.

4. Rowan berries

This berry is a product of the Rowan or Mountain Ash. It is, in fact, a tree which
is known to grow to at least ten meters tall! However, it can often be found as a
large bush. It is a common sight along the side of the road and in parks as well as

waste ground. The bark is grey whilst the leaves are lance shaped; usually consisting of three pairs of lance shapes.

The Rowan berry is bright red and small; it has a circumference of just eight millimeters. It is also an exceptional sour berry. It will absorb the moisture from your mouth and leave you feeling dry and sour. However, it can be added to a recipe to create a delicious jelly, the sourness is removed during the cooking process with the aid of sugar. If you have a little more time you can even make rowan berry wine although this typically takes a year to properly mature.

5. The Autumn Olive

http://msue.anr.msu.edu/uploads/images/12-1%20autumn%20olive%20GRETCHEN.jpg

This is another red berry which appears in the autumn and can be used for a variety of purposes. The plant appears as a shrub but can grow as high as fifteen feet if left alone in the wild! The leaves have a silvery effect contrasting against the red berries to create a stunning backdrop in almost any setting.

The leaves on this shrub are oblong and have smooth edges; green on top and the silvery color underneath. It is also worth noting that they appear alternately on a long brown twig; checking the leaves are alternating will ensure you have an autumn berry and not confused them with something else, such as a honeysuckle berry.

The berry does have a small stone inside it which must be removed before you can eat it as it is big enough to potentially make you choke.

It is possible to collect these berries in August but only if they have been in full sun. Most shrubs are partially in the shade and will not ripen until the end of September. The longer you leave the berries the sweeter they become but the more desirable they become to birds so they may be harder to find.

If the berries are ripe you should be able to run your finger across a branch and the berries will literally drop into your hand. Whilst you can pit them and eat them raw they are often used to make delicious jams and pies.

Chapter 3 – 5 Other Common Autumnal Foraging Foods

The range of food it is possible to find growing in the wild at this time of year is impressive. You will be able to find something interesting and edible within a short distance of your home. In fact, the more you look the more you will find potentially edible fruits, berries and nuts all around you. Once you have sampled the delights of collecting, preparing and consuming your own food you will almost certainly become addicted.

Even some of the most commonly seen fruits sold in supermarkets can be had for free at this time of year.

1. Apples

The apple is a stable fruit for many households; it is also a product which is freely available on many streets. The humble apple tree has become a popular edition to gardens and parks across the world. It is also found in many woods and forests; simply because of the abundant popularity of this tree.

You may even discover that there is an abandoned orchard near you! They appear everywhere as one discarded apple core can produce several trees. It is fairly obvious when an apple is ripe and ready to be eaten; in fact, they will start falling to the ground and even these can be consumed. The only thing to watch for is the tell tale mark of a worm or caterpillar; this is guaranteed to ruin your eating experience.

The best way to assess an apple is simply to taste it. If it is a little sour then it is likely to be a cooking apple, sweet and delicious equals an eating apple. Any cooking apple can be used to make apple sauce, apple jelly, wine or even cider.

2. *Giant Puffball*

This is a type of mushroom and you should be careful to ensure you have the right one before you consume it. Fortunately this is the easiest one for anyone to identify. It is commonly found in many parts of Europe and northern America. As you would imagine it is a large white ball shaped fungi. It looks very similar to a football. It will be soft to the touch but when cut open you should see a solid white color inside. If it is not then you either have the wrong mushroom or it is past the edible stage. Having said that it is very difficult to confuse this with any other type of mushroom; it is unique. They can be found in the middle of fields or along the edges of hedges, all they require is damp soil and some sunlight. Wet conditions are best for all mushrooms.

To eat you can slice the puffball up and fry it in garlic butter. It is also possible to freeze the slices and use them in the future when you are in the mood for a giant puffball.

3. Rosehip

This fruit is an excellent alternative to the usual citrus fruits. This was particularly true during the Second World War when food was rationed and many foreign fruits were hard to obtain. The Rosehip grows naturally in abundance in the hedgerows, fields, woods and even rough grassland across all parts of Europe and America. This makes it an excellent choice for a variety of purposes.

The plant can grow as high as ten foot tall and the leaves are distinctive as they are formed in toothed pairs. It will have pink or white flowers and the actual fruit is oblong and an orange / red color. The plant does have thorns which you should be careful to avoid and the seeds inside the Rosehips should be removed before you consume them. They are known to be full of vitamin C and can be crushed to extract the juice which can add flavor to almost any meal.

However, it is important to remove the hairs which are on the outside of the Rosehips, these can be extremely irritating. To do this it is best to pick them wearing gloves and then strain them through a jelly bag. You can then make the syrup or even use them to create a delicious jelly. They are an excellent accompaniment to ginger, almonds, and even lemon. The Swedes have even been known to make a soup from the rosehip.

4. *Chicken of the Woods*

This is another very distinctive type of fungus which can often be found on the side or near the base of a dead or dying Oak tree, it is also found in other hard wood trees which are near the end of their lives. It has a bright orange appearance and looks like it has grown as several shelves stacked on top of each other. It is referred to as the chicken of the woods as it tastes very similar to chicken and even has a similar texture. It is often used by vegetarians as a substitute for chicken in risottos or stews.

Unfortunately this delicious type of fungi is only really found in North America. The flesh is thick but soft and watery when the fungus is young; as it matures the flesh hardens and eventually becomes crumbly. The insides are a pale yellow or white color. It is worth noting that a small number of people have a reaction to this type of fungi, although it is safe to eat. It is therefore essential that you taste a small amount first to ensure you are not one of the unfortunate ones.

5. Raspberries

The final selection of all the available fruits and berries that can be foraged naturally is the humble raspberry. This can be grown in your garden although it will spread quickly and can take over far more of your garden than you initially intended. The raspberry is a soft red berry which starts to ripen at the end of August but can be picked right through to mid October. Like so many plants the actual time of ripening will be affected by the position of the plant and the amount of sun it receives.

The Raspberry can be eaten as soon as it has been picked, in common with the blackberry a simple gentle downwards twist should free a ripe raspberry from its plant and, if you find a good bush, you should be able to collect a significant quantity in a short space of time. Raspberries can be found almost anywhere as they are often planted by homeowners and the ease in which they spread means they are prevalent in woods as well as rough grasslands.

Once picked you should soak the berries to remove any small bugs; you can then either freeze them or turn them into a delicious pie, crumble or even eat them with yoghurt or cream; The berry is already sweet and needs no additional sugar making it the perfect addition to almost any recipe.

A Few Tips for Successful Foraging

To successfully forage you should always carry a notebook and pen to record any potential sites. As already mentioned the appropriate clothing will help to ensure you do not get scratched, stung or affected by poison ivy. However, there are several other tips which can help you to make a success of your foraging missions:

- Know your area – It is important to know what fruits, berries and nuts should be available within the area you live. Your climate and environment will affect the selection available. Knowing what to find will ensure you are looking for something that it is possible to find.

- Respect – The first rule of foraging is not to damage property or other plants whilst collecting your harvest. You should also only ever harvest what you need for yourself. Do not take too much as this will prevent other foragers from enjoying the experience and will damage future harvests.

- Try it – Never be afraid to try something new; there are many delicious natural items to be found. However, if you are at all unsure regarding a specific item then do not chance it. Take one berry or a picture and consult a friend or expert before picking and consuming them. Once you have discovered edible items try them in as many different recipes and methods of eating as possible.

- Take a friend – Whenever you forage it is advisable to have someone else with you. Not only will you be able to share your knowledge you will both have a back-up if something goes wrong and you need to get help.

Conclusion

Foraging for food is a rewarding and exciting opportunity to become more in touch with the natural world around you. It is also an excellent opportunity to get your family out and about exploring nature and completing fun activities together. It is certainly an experience you will want to repeat once you have started it!

Once you decide to search for food in your local area it is important to prepare yourself properly first. The right clothing has already been mentioned. However, one of the most important aspects of foraging is knowing where to go. As you build your experience you will record your favorite spots and even target your preferred food products. However, in the beginning it is advisable to seek as much assistance as possible. You can do this by exploring your local area and keeping your eyes open. A more effective way can often be established by contacting other people who have already gained experience as foragers. These people can be contacted via social media sites; you may even find that there is a local club! Providing you are respectful of the environment and do not over harvest these sites, these people will be happy to share their experiences. You may learn much more than you expect to!

It is also possible to plant your own food sources. Whilst many nuts and products which grow on trees will take many years to come to fruition, smaller plants, particularly the blackberry, raspberry, strawberry or even gooseberry bush can provide a harvest within a few years. This will never replace you foraging trips but it will increase the food you can access, especially if time is limited.

Finding food for free, whether you live in a city or a rural area is possible and deeply satisfying. It provides a feeling similar to the classic hunter who has tracked down and captured their desired prey. It is also a useful skill. The more you practice foraging the more you will learn and the better able you will be to provide for yourself should you ever become lost or trapped in the wilderness. Foraging is more than just a fun pastime; it can actually be a lifesaving skill.

On the lighter side it is an excellent opportunity for family bonding and encouraging your children to have an active interest in the world around them and the capabilities of Mother Nature to sustain them; as was common in ancient times. It also allows you the opportunity to control the foods you and your family are eating. You will be less exposed to processed foods and more appreciative of nature.

FREE Bonus Reminder

If you have not grabbed it yet, please go ahead and download your special bonus E book *"Chakras for Beginners. 7 Steps To Understand And Balance Chakras, Radiate Energy, And Strengthen Aura"*.

Simply Click the Button Below

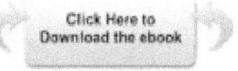

OR Go to This Page

http://lifehacksworld.com/free

BONUS #2: More Free & Discounted Books & Products

Do you want to receive more Free/Discounted Books or Products?

We have a mailing list where we send out our new Books or Products when they go free or with a discount on Amazon. Click on the link below to sign up for Free & Discount Book & Product Promotions.

=> Sign Up for Free & Discount Book & Product Promotions <=

OR Go to this URL

http://zbit.ly/1WBb1Ek

www.ingramcontent.com/pod-product-compliance
Lightning Source LLC
Chambersburg PA
CBHW071324280526
45788CB00004B/2005